Tractors at Work

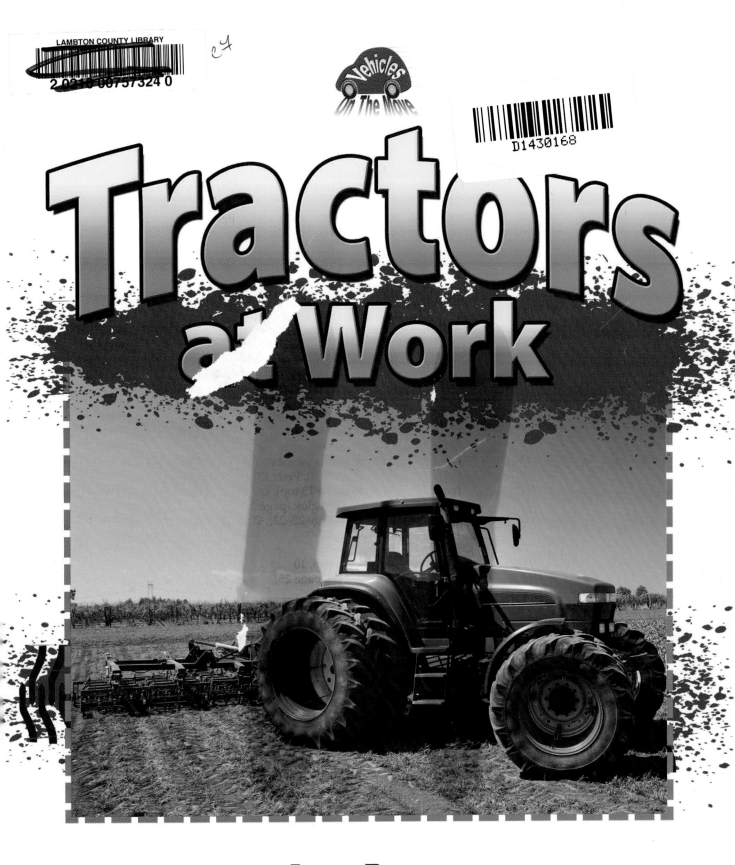

Lynn Peppas

🌿 Crabtree Publishing Company

www.crabtreebooks.com

Created by Bobbie Kalman

Dedicated By Crystal Sikkens
To the Sikkens family for introducing me to farm life

Author
Lynn Peppas

Editorial director
Kathy Middleton

Project editor
Paul Challen

Editor
Adrianna Morganelli

Proofreaders
Rachel Stuckey
Reagan Miller

Photo research
Melissa McClellan

Design
Tibor Choleva

Production coordinators
Katherine Berti
Margaret Amy Salter

Prepress technicians
Katherine Berti
Margaret Amy Salter

Consultant
Mary Dawson, Farm Equipment Sales Representative

Special thanks to
Jonathan Sikkens

Illustrations
All illustrations by Leif Peng

Photographs
Dreamstime.com: © Gualtiero Boffi (pages 4, 7); © Olga D. Van De Veer (page 5); © Sharon Agar (page 12–13); © Marcin Husiatynski (pages 16–17, 17 top); © Gordana Sermek (page 18); © Uatp1 (page 26); © Ovidiu Iordache (page 27)
istockphoto.com: © RonBailey (page 19); © HHakim (page 28); © buzbuzzer (page 31)
Shutterstock.com: © Krivosheev Vitaly (front cover); © dusko (title page); © Dusan Bartolovic (page 8); Peter Zijlstra (page 9); © Marilyn Barbone (page 11); © Inginsh (page 13 top); © Alekcey (pages 14, 24); © Orientaly (page 15); © Leonid Shcheglov (page 20); © Konstantin Sutyagin (page 21); © Losevsky Pavel (page 22–23); © Serghei Starus (page 29); © Neil Phillip Mey (page 30)
© Stu Harrding: page 23
© Melissa McClellan: pages 6, 10
Public Domain: back cover, page 25

Library and Archives Canada Cataloguing in Publication

Peppas, Lynn
        Tractors at work / Lynn Peppas.

(Vehicles on the move)
Includes index.
Issued also in an electronic format.
ISBN 978-0-7787-3050-7 (bound).--ISBN 978-0-7787-3064-4 (pbk.)

        1. Tractors--Juvenile literature. I. Title. II. Series: Vehicles on the move

TL233.15.P46 2011   j629.225'2   C2010-904804-0

Library of Congress Cataloging-in-Publication Data

CIP available at Library of Congress

C. +

Crabtree Publishing Company

Printed in the U.S.A./082010/BA20100709

www.crabtreebooks.com   1-800-387-7650

Published in Canada
Crabtree Publishing
616 Welland Ave.
St. Catharines, ON
L2M 5V6

Published in the United States
Crabtree Publishing
PMB 59051
350 Fifth Avenue, 59th Floor
New York, New York 10118

Published in the United Kingdom
Crabtree Publishing
Maritime House
Basin Road North, Hove
BN41 1WR

Published in Australia
Crabtree Publishing
386 Mt. Alexander Rd.
Ascot Vale (Melbourne)
VIC 3032

Contents

Hard-working tractors

Tractors are hard-working **vehicles**. Vehicles are machines that can move and do work. Tractors work hard to do many kinds of jobs. They can move on different types of surfaces. They push and pull equipment and heavy loads. They get the job done!

Tractors collecting hay bales on a big farm

All kinds of work

No job is too small or too big for a tractor. Smaller tractors mow large lawns and care for large gardens. Larger tractors work on farms or construction sites. The size of the tractor depends on the work that needs to be done.

Small tractors can be used to mow large lawns.

Tractor power

Tractors have heavy-duty engines that give them a lot of power. A tractor's motor is in the front. Its power is measured in **horsepower**. One horsepower can carry 33,000 pounds (15,000 kg) over one foot (30 cm) in one minute.

engine

Tractors need a lot of power to pull equipment like plows, cultivators, and mowers, and to push snowplows and diggers.

side view mirror

cab

6930

engine

headlights

back wheel

front wheel

This tractor can do the work of 120 horses!

Slow and steady

Tractors have **traction**. Traction means that they can move heavy loads on any kind of surface. Tractors cannot travel very fast like cars can. But they can do heavy work on bumpy or muddy surfaces. Cars could never do that!

Wheeling around

Many tractors have four-wheel drive. That means that the engine powers each wheel on its own. This helps tractors work on muddy or rocky surfaces. Slow and steady really does get the job done!

Traction and four-wheel drive help this tractor pull the plow across muddy fields.

Hitchin' a ride

A tractor pulls other machines that do work. It has a **hitch** in the back called a three-point hitch. Machines attach to the tractor by the hitch.

three-point hitch

power take-off

Powering up

Some machines pulled by a tractor need power to run, such as a **hay baler**. The power take-off on a tractor, also called the PTO, gives machines the power they need. Machines connect to the power take-off in the middle of the hitch. They draw power from the tractor's engine.

a closer look

hay baler connected to the PTO

Front-end jobs

Tractors lift and push from the front. **Front-end loaders** have arms at the front. These arms attach to forks or buckets. Tractors scoop and lift many kinds of heavy loads.

arms

bucket

Snow blade

Tractors push loads, too. Heavy-duty blades attach to the front. They push dirt or sometimes snow in the winter.

blade

a bale of hay

arms attached to forks

Big wheels

Big tires help a tractor move on soft, muddy surfaces. Tires are made of rubber. They have deep **treads**, or patterns, that grip the surface. Some treads are over six inches (15 cm) deep. Some tires are taller than a person standing.

deep tire treads

Many wheels in action

Tractors are heavy vehicles. A tractor's big wheels carry its weight over a large area. Big wheels help make sure a tractor does not crush the soil or crops. Some tractors have 4, 6, 8, or even 12 wheels!

Powerful tractors with many wheels are used on big farms.

Big eight-wheeled tractors can easily pull large plows and other farm machines.

Making tracks

Some tractors move on **tracks** instead of tires. These are called **crawler tractors**. The tracks are made of rubber and have deep treads. Some crawler tractors have two tracks. Some have four smaller ones.

engine

tracks

Crawling along

Crawler tractors easily drive over any kind of surface. The heavy weight of the tractor is carried over a larger area than tires. This means they do less harm to soil and crops.

a two-track tractor

cab

a four-track tractor

CUT-out for smaller jobs

CUT stands for **compact utility tractor**. A CUT is smaller in size but still does a lot of different jobs. It can move and turn easier than larger tractors, too. CUTs are perfect for working on golf courses or large homes with gardens and yards. A CUT's engine is between 20 and 50 horsepower.

This CUT is pushing a golf ball collector on a driving range.

Attached and ready!

CUTs have a hitch and PTO just like regular-sized tractors. Machines such as **posthole diggers** attach to these compact tractors. This machine digs holes for fence posts. Mowers attached to a CUT are used to cut large lawns such as parks and golf courses.

Posthole diggers can be attached to many different tractors.

This farm worker is digging a hole with a posthole digger attached to a tractor.

Utility farm tractors

Utility tractors are regular-sized tractors used on farms. They pull heavy equipment and loads behind them. Weights are added to the front of the tractor or to the tractor's wheels to help it pull these heavy loads.

Front-end weights help with traction, stability, and safety.

Hi-tech helpers

Tractors have rollover bars to keep drivers safe.
Some have computers that tell the driver how much
work has been done. Computers let drivers switch
from one job to another without stopping.

rollover bar

front-end weights

Even tractors without cabs can have rollover bars to protect drivers if the tractor tips over.

Monster tractors

Really big farms have thousands of acres of crops. They need monster tractors to get their jobs done. Monster tractors have really big engines that can pull very large loads and machines. These tractors can have 200 to 900 horsepower engines.

Now that's big!

The world's largest tractor is called the Big Bud 747. It has over a 900 horsepower engine. It weighs 130,000 pounds (59,000 kg) and is 14 feet (four m) high. Some of its wheels are over eight feet (2.5 m) tall.

Backhoe

Not all tractors work on farms. Some work on construction sites, too. A **backhoe** is a type of tractor that is useful in both places. The front of a backhoe has a bucket called a loader. This bucket is used for lifting and moving heavy loads of dirt or stones.

stabilizer bar

joints

boom

cab

loader

bucket

Hoe, hoe, hoe...

The back has a hoe that is used for digging. It has a powerful arm with a smaller bucket on the end. The bucket has prongs, or teeth that help it dig. The driver has a seat that swivels, or turns. The driver can face frontward or backward in the cab of the backhoe.

Backhoes are very useful machines. They can be used for many jobs, including removing old tree stumps.

Bulldozer

A **bulldozer** is another tractor that is useful at construction sites. Bulldozers are usually crawler tractors with tracks instead of wheels.

engine

blade

cab

tracks

ripper

Looking sharp

A bulldozer has a heavy, metal blade on its front. This blade is used for pushing soil or gravel. There is a **ripper** in the back. This is a tool with a sharp claw that can break up rock and very hard dirt surfaces.

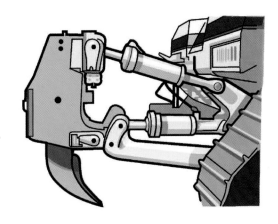

Rippers at the back of bulldozers can be used to break up old pavements on roads and sidewalks.

Pushback tractors

A **pushback tractor** works at an airport. It is a powerful vehicle that pushes passenger aircraft away from the airport terminal. Pushback tractors are sometimes called tugs. They are flat on top, and low to the ground. They fit underneath big airplanes.

Pushing it

Pushback tractors are heavy. Their heavy weight gives them extra traction. Some weigh more than 59 tons (54 metric tons). Some pushback tractors have a towbar that connects to the front wheels of the aircraft.

Pushback tractors have powerful engines that can push heavy airplanes and other loads.

Tractor pulls

Tractor pull competitions are held all around the world. Tractors try to pull the most weight for the longest distance. Tractors pull a metal sled with weights on it. Weights can go up to 65,000 pounds (29,000 kg). Tractor pulls are usually held on dirt track surfaces in large or outdoor arenas.

Ready, set...pull!

Sometimes, regular working tractors compete.
Some tractors are specially made for tractor pull
competitions. They have more than one engine.
Some even have jet engines!

Small lawn tractors compete in races, too. There are different classes of tractors.
Racers as young as ten years old can compete in lawn tractor competitions.

Words to know and Index

backhoe
pages 24–25

Compact Utility Tractor
pages 18–19

crawler tractors
pages 16–17, 24

Front-end loaders
pages 12–13

hay baler
page 11

posthole digger
page 19

pushback tractor
pages 28–29

ripper
page 27